Being Cooperative

Way to Be!

by Jill Lynn Donahue   illustrated by Stacey Previn

PICTURE WINDOW BOOKS
Minneapolis, Minnesota

Special thanks to our advisers for their expertise:

Kay Augustine
National Director and Character Education Specialist, Ignite
West Des Moines, Iowa

Terry Flaherty, Ph.D., Professor of English
Minnesota State University, Mankato

Editor: Shelly Lyons
Designer: Tracy Davies
Page Production: Melissa Kes
Art Director: Nathan Gassman
Associate Managing Editor: Christianne Jones
The illustrations in this book were created with acrylics.

Picture Window Books
5115 Excelsior Boulevard
Suite 232
Minneapolis, MN 55416
877-845-8392
www.picturewindowbooks.com

Printed in the United States of America.

All books published by Picture Window Books
are manufactured with paper containing at least
10 percent post-consumer waste.

Library of Congress Cataloging-in-Publication Data
Donahue, Jill L. (Jill Lynn), 1967-
Being cooperative / by Jill Lynn Donahue ;
illustrated by Stacey Previn.
p. cm. — (Way to be!)
Includes bibliographical references and index.
ISBN-13: 978-1-4048-3779-9 (library binding)
ISBN-10: 1-4048-3779-5 (library binding)
1. Cooperativeness—Juvenile literature. I. Previn, Stacey.
II. Title.
BJ1533.C74D66 2008
179'.9–dc22   2007004589

Being cooperative means working with others as a group. People who work together can often get things done better and faster than someone who works alone. Cooperative people know that by doing their part, everyone is better off.

One weekend, Morgan asks families to clean up the neighborhood park. They pick up trash and plant trees and flowers.

The families are being cooperative.

5

There are many leaves in Maya's yard. Maya's family members work together to rake up the leaves.

Maya's family members are being cooperative.

During the school show, each student holds up a letter. The letters spell out a special message for the students' parents.

The students are being cooperative.

Max is trying to build a big snow fort.
Max's friends add snowballs so they
can all hide behind the fort.

**Max and his friends are
being cooperative.**

At recess, seven friends want to ride the merry-go-round.
The friends all take turns pushing.

The friends are being cooperative.

Tom's cat, Tiger, runs out of the house. Tom's brother and sister help look for Tiger.

Tom, his brother, and his sister are being cooperative.

Sue makes silly puppets. Carson writes a funny story. Together they will put on a great puppet show for their parents.

Sue and Carson are being cooperative.

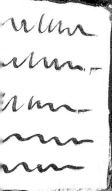

Layla and her friends find a big branch on the bike trail. They all help pull the branch off the trail.

Layla and her friends are being cooperative.

19

In art class, each student paints a small part
of a picture. All of the parts together make
a big, beautiful picture called a mural.

**The students are
being cooperative.**

Four friends want to have a lemonade stand. Each one of them brings something they will need.

The friends are being cooperative.

To Learn More

At the Library

Mahoney, Daniel J. *The Perfect Clubhouse.* New York: Clarion Books, 2004.

Riehecky, Janet. *Cooperation.* Mankato, Minn.: Capstone Press, 2005.

Scheunemann, Pam. *Working Together.* Edina, Minn.: ABDO Publishing Co., 2004.

On the Web

FactHound offers a safe, fun way to find Web sites related to this book.
All of the sites on FactHound have been researched by our staff.

1. Visit www.facthound.com
2. Type in this special code: 1404837795
3. Click on the FETCH IT button.

Your trusty FactHound will fetch the best sites for you!

Index

Look for all of the books in the Way to Be! series: